Levities: Witticisms and Absurdities in Verse, Second Edition

Levities and Gravities, Second Edition, Volume 1

Benjamin Cannicott Shavitz

Published by Benjamin Cannicott Shavitz, 2023.

LEVITIES: WITTICISMS AND ABSURDITIES IN VERSE, SECOND EDITION

First edition. June 19, 2023.

ISBN: 979-8223339090

Written by Benjamin Cannicott Shavitz.

Table of Contents

For Truth

INTRODUCTION

This volume is a collection of humorous and light poetry. It is part of the author's Levities and Gravities project. The Levities and Gravities project demonstrates the power of linguistic form in poetry and highlights the fact that poetry can evoke any emotion, whether light or heavy. This volume contains "levities," or humorous or light poems, but the companion volume, *Gravities*, presents serious poems. This second edition contains additional poems not included in the first edition, new author's notes, and an essay on the possibilities available in poetry.

THE AUTHOR

Benjamin Cannicott Shavitz holds an M. A., an MPhil, and a PhD in linguistics from The City University of New York and previously taught The Structure of Modern English and The History of the English Language at Hunter College in Manhattan, New York City. Since linguists understand language to be the pairing of form and meaning, Ben's poetry engages not only with meaning but with the aspects of linguistic form, including prosody (meter), phonological patterns (e. g., rhyme, alliteration, sound class patterning), and translanguaging and dialectal phenomena (e. g., varying and mixing dialects and languages). Ben's training in the structure of language affords him technical control over the form of his poems, allowing for infinite design possibilities. Ben also holds a B. A. in multidisciplinary studies from Stony Brook University, which covers concentrations in engineering, English, and linguistics, as well as peripheral studies in numerous other areas. Ben's broad knowledge base fuels the subject matter of his poems and he thus writes on a wide range of topics. Ben's poem "Before the Fall" (not included in the Levities and Gravities series) is set to be published in an upcoming edition of the poetry magazine *The Lyric*. Ben was born in 1993 in Manhattan, New York City where he still resides. For more of Ben's work and poetry, view www.kingsfieldendeavors.com[1].

---

1. http://www.kingsfieldendeavors.com

There is many a trained gnoseologist
Who has lectured at numerous colleges
Unto whom you can listen
Parse kennen from wissen
And emerge without knowing what knowledge is.

Author's Note: A "gnoseologist" is a practitioner of gnoseology, the study of knowledge. "Kennen" and "wissen" are German verbs with different meanings that both translate into English as "to know." "Kennen" means "to know" in the sense of "to be acquainted with," like when you know a person. "Wissen" means "to know" in the sense of "to hold as information in the mind," like when you know a fact.

We're both so busy, it's a crime.
I think I'd only know you'd died
If, when you fin'lly had the time,
You texted from the other side.

Advertisement

So you've found yourself stuck in a well
And it's deep and it's dark and you're scared
And you just don't know what's to be done.
Well, the first thing is get yourself out
And the next's, grab some scones. Two for one!

Well, writing some dog'rel
To mark the inog'rel
Just isn't as hard as it seems like.
You scrawl stuff at random,
Then stitch it up tandem
And mention what all the regime's like.

Just write about heroes
And dollars with zeros
And gen'rally write about winning.
It all goes quite splendid
And none leaves offended
And all of the faces are grinning.

I feel convinced the world is fine
When I am double-fisting wine.
But only then. Is that a sign?
No. I will not pursue that line
Of thinking.
I'm drinking.

Alternate Timeline

Author's Note: This poem is an exercise in what sociolinguists might call deliberate translanguaging, except, instead of interweaving different languages to form a new way of speaking, it mixes two very different dialects of English: NYC AAE (New York City African American English, the main non-standard dialect spoken by my childhood friends and peers) and Scots (the most colloquial Scottish English dialect, a dialect I have studied for professional purposes as a linguist). The poem's narrative explains how the new dialect the poem is written in might have originated by laying out an alternate timeline that could have begun in 2020, given the following historical context: For decades, New York City has been undergoing gentrification and rents have increased to the point that they are now notoriously high; in 2014, nearly 45 percent of Scottish voters voted for independence from the United Kingdom; in 2020, the United States witnessed massive protests against oppressive treatment of black Americans, including many demonstrations in New York City; and, also in 2020, the United Kingdom left the European Union despite large-scale opposition in Scotland. This poem creates a whole new way of talking with a backstory to go with it!

Original Dialect:
Yo, gin y'a' dinna kin what's good,
Ain't seen our Afro-Scottish 'hood,
Then y'a' gon' listen to the tawe
'Nint how we settud Tubmandawe.

In 2020, Britain dipped
Fae Europe. Syne the Scottish flipped.
In parliamint, they lost it: "Weew!
Y'a' didna fuck wif how we feew.

So dinna fash 'nint us no more.
We out. We gangin' thoo thon door.

And no the morra — straight-up na.
We vote to bounce, thin we awa."

They did anaw, un-U'd the K.
The Scottish peaced aud Bess that day.
And quat o daft-ass southron law,
That Scotland life was aye mad braw.

But, tween hands, Harlem rents was lang.
America was racist, wrang,
And blauded black fowk ilka hour.
Thon joint'd no e'en thowe black power.

The Bronx-and-Harlem black fowk sighed,
"We down for somebit new to bide.
A pairt where iwkane wishin' us
To bide there, dinna say we sus,

Where fowk no spittin', 'Y'a' gang hyne,
Y'a' sleekit, no-kin-nothin' swine.'
But that a bonnie fairy tawe.
Where we gon' gang? We canna baiw."

But, braw or busted, nothin' haud
For aye; the weather hot thin caud.
Thim Scots fowk bumpin' rager'd no
Gang forrit mor'n a monf or so.

'Cause, in a wee, they parliamint
Come buggin' to the fowk anint,
"We dinna gat 'nough citizins.
Athoot them southrons, we just glins.

We needin' more fowk bidin' here.
'Cause, ithergates, we'n last ae year."
And so, the Scots, athort the earf,
Was seekin' fowk that wished rebirf.

The Scots was seekin' fowk who's no
Yet down to thowe the busted flow
Of where they was, who'd saiw athort
The earf to cleek a chiller port.

The black New Yorkers seen they tid
And claucht it sicker what they did:
"Yo, Scotland fowk, we 'nint thon life
Wif lown, athoot no fash and strife!"

Syne, half a million black fowk dipped
Fae New York City, up and shipped
Theysewves athort the muckuw sea
And primed our howe thoo Scotch decree.

So black New Yorkers makkit thim
A ballin' town; they didna slim:
They bug a bumpin' market-stead
Wif muckle scowf and gat ahead.

We bidin' yet, four decades syne,
In Tubmandawe, no gettin' "swine."
And why our howe get Tubmandawe?
'Cause Tubman sayed, "Flit norf. Let's baiw!"

* * *

Translation:
Hey you, if you all don't know what's going on,

Haven't seen our Afro-Scottish neighborhood,
Then you're all going to listen to the tale
About how we settled Tubmandale.

In 2020, Britain left
From Europe. Soon after, the Scottish people freaked out.
In Parliament, they lost it: "Well!
You all didn't consider how we feel.

So don't worry about us anymore.
We're leaving. We're going through that door.
And not tomorrow — right now.
We vote to leave, then we go."

They did too, un-U(nit)ed the K(ingdom).
The Scottish said goodbye to old Elizabeth (II) that day.
And free from crazy English law,
Life in Scotland was always extremely good.

But, meanwhile, Harlem rents were high.
America was racist, wrong
And injured black people every hour.
That place would not even endure black power.

The Bronx-and-Harlem black people sighed,
"We would be interested in someplace new to live.
An area where everyone wants us
To live there, don't say we're suspicious,

Where people aren't saying, 'You all leave here,
You untrustworthy, know-nothing swine.'
But that's a pretty fairy tale.
Where are we going to go? We cannot leave."

But excellent or broken, nothing lasts
Forever; the weather's hot then cold.
The Scottish people's raucous party wouldn't
Go on more than a month or so.

Because, in a short time, their parliament
Came around freaking out to the people about,
"We don't have enough citizens.
Without the English, we're just glens.

We need more people living here.
Because, otherwise, we're going to last one year."
And so the Scots, across the earth,
Were seeking people who wanted rebirth.

The Scots were seeking people who weren't
Still satisfied to endure the broken nature
Of where they were, who'd sail across
The earth to seize a less troubled port.

The black New Yorkers saw the opportunity
And seized it firmly is what they did:
"Hey Scottish people, we're interested in that life
With peace, without any concern or strife!"

Soon after, half a million black people left
From New York City, shipped
Themselves across the vast sea
And filled our valley through Scottish decree.

So black New Yorkers made themselves
A prosperous town; they didn't treat their work carelessly:
They built a thriving market town
With a lot of freedom and got ahead.

We're living still, four decades later
In Tubmandale, not being called "swine."
And why is our valley called Tubmandale?
Because (Harriet) Tubman said, "Move north. Let's leave!"

Now if you will remember the Alamo, friend,
Well, then I will remember the Maine.
'Cause it's very important we harbor a grudge
Against Mexican soldiers and Spain.
Though their governments now're not the same as back then,
We must cling to historical ire.
'Cause if we're not in danger from foreign attacks,
We can't panic like everything's dire
And can't buy these cool weapons to fire!

Your race is but a construct and your gender made-up roles.
Your culture and your country are but thoughts your peers install.
The substance that defines you is your talent and your goals.
Well, then again, your height exists, so beat it if you're small.

Left jab. Clean dodge. Right jab. Straight miss.
Spot Guy by Pickup Taking Piss.
Left hook. Too soft. Right hook. Spilled beer!
He's mad now and the bros all cheer.
He swings. I duck. He misses, but
My falling jaw hits uppercut.
I hit the pavement. World's a blot.
Oh what a life, the parking lot!

America the Beautiful: An Update

O beautiful for parking lots,
For needless asphalt plains,
Environmental liver spots,
Vast sloth-supporting stains.

America! America!
We purchase our decline!
In cars we trust to help us rust
And thus self-undermine.

O beautiful for suburbs, these
Vain ant farms for our cars,
Where not a soul another sees,
Except at zoned bazaars.

America! America!
God paint each picket fence
That every heart beat far apart
At humankind's expense.

O beautiful for urban sprawl,
Built wide instead of high,
Where concepts like "adjoining wall"
And "sidewalk" go to die.

America! America!
Here Jesus drives a truck.
He used to care that people share,
But backseats say, "I suck."

O beautiful for interstates,

Most varicose of veins,
Where every heart each other hates
For slowing down the lanes.

America! America!
I-5 or LIE,
Each battlefield where none will yield
'S where life is truly free.

It must be awkward for a god to pray for the persistence
Of worship from a shrinking flock whose prayers bring his existence.

Oh, God, to be oppressed!
Just think of all the glory to be had.
To be by heaven blessed,
Incapable of actions wrong or bad!
So pure that no one ever could be mad!
Oh, that would be the best.

Belief

God's the creator of all of humanity
Or he's the product of man's group insanity.
You can decide with your own will and brain
But remember that you, once again, are insane.

The funny thing with Jesus Christ
Is Pontius Pilate had him iced.
The Romans did it, not the Jews.
Should someone tell the pope the news?

Hey, why'd I buy that second yacht?
I think I knew, but I forgot.

I'm the queen of yellow.
You're the king of red.
You're a handsome fellow.
Orange lies ahead.

"I really wanna travel, bro."
"Of course. So where you wanna go?"
"But that's the thing, man. I don't know."
"Well, you could try to make a plan.
You think like France or more Japan
Or somewhere kinda Pakistan?"
"It's Pockiston, bro. How you sound?
Know culture. It's, like, mad profound.
You gotta do the work, my man
And *please* go buy that other round."

To honor Christ, the sinless child
Who brought Earth peace and mercy mild,
We'll crank the jams to get us riled
And drink until the floor is tiled
With rows of passersout whose bile'd
Concern us were we not beguiled
By knowledge we'll be reconciled
With God and stand re-undefiled
On Christmas morning. Life is wild.

If Jesus was for real for real,
He'd have — at least — a sneaker deal.

What I actually read aloud in German (the first stanza of Schiller's An Die Freude/ Beethoven's Ode to Joy):

Freude, schöner Götterfunken,
Tochter aus Elysium,
Wir betreten feuertrunken,
Himmlische, dein Heiligtum.
Deine Zauber binden wieder,
Was die Mode streng geteilt,
Alle Menschen werden Brüder,
Wo dein sanfter Flügel weilt.
Seid umschlungen, Millionen!
Diesen Kuss der ganzen Welt!
Brüder—überm Sternenzelt
Muss ein lieber Vater wohnen.

What my speech-to-text software thought I said because it was expecting English:

Roll a die good night good function.
Dr. House Azizi womb.
View Bill Clinton oh yeah pumpkin.
Henley shirt dime high leg tomb.
Dinah sober Ben Ben be there.
Plus Komodo strangle tile.
Allah mansion wear them please there.
Go dine John staff Smeagol dial.
Side comb Slomin's Millie Onan.
Diesel goose dare guns and belt.
Blue bear eBay standing cell.
Moonshine Libra bob hair ronin.

Zey Are skinnY and wEAr ze brIght and pInk tutUs.
Zey Are, for sOme reasOn, ze One sing I can Use
To — qu'Est-ce que c'Est? — functiOn wissIn ma lIfe as mUse.
Ze Art's paintEd by mOI. FetIsh I dO not chOOse.
Mais c'Est la vIE.

Author's Note: The capitalized vowels in this poem indicate where the stress is supposed to be placed. These stress positions are not natural to English, but they are where a native French speaker with a strong French accent in English would place the stresses because stress in French is generally placed on the final syllable of a word. As Edgar Degas, the famous painter of ballerinas, was French, this accent seems appropriate.

It's feminine to use the stove.
It's masculine to use the grill.
I don't quite think I understand.
I'm not quite sure I ever will.

Marriage will thrive if respect can attach you, but
It can be helpful if you have a statue butt.

Crappy Thought
(On Robert Louis Stevenson's "Happy Thought")

The world is so full of a number of things,
I'm sure we should all be as happy as kings,
But, since we are not, it is prudent to add
That most of those things are confusing or bad.

Author's Note: The first two lines of this poem are the entirety of Robert Louis Stevenson's poem "Happy Thought" verbatim. The other two lines are my addition.

He's a sexy ignoramus,
So, of course, he's super famous.

Crusade

On Crusade in the land of the Saracen
And on leave from their virtuous garrison,
Footmen Roberts and Morehouse
Encountered a whorehouse.
"Well, it certainly would be embarrassin'
If," said Roberts, "we entered this lair o' sin.
For although it would ease us,
We're fighting for Jesus."
"Don't," said Morehouse, while ent'ring, "beware o' sin.
For each pagan we kill, we repair a sin.
All our merciless slaying
Is stronger than praying
At repelling what lust might ensnare us in."

I'll convert to your religion
If you're lithe and callipygian.

Author's Note: "Callipygian" is an adjective meaning "having beautiful buttocks."

It doesn't become you to act like new money.
You'd trace back as far as an Astor'd.
This popping of bottles of cava's not funny.
You're meant to be *secretly* plastered.

We cain't have folks with melanin residin' as our neighbors,
Cain't be no blacks ner Mexicans within our white-man spaces.
But someone's gotta carry out the least enticin' labors.
We need, then, low-cost workers from the purest, palest places.
Y'all know, folks, what we gotta do: let's call the army's legions
And launch platoons off northward to enslave us some Norwegians.

I seldom hear a word of news
That makes the world seem good.
The righteous always seem to lose
When you don't think they should.

This horror never seems to change.
I hope it never will,
For, though that may sound rather strange,
The Times has goods to shill.

Eloquence

He murdered his wife with a hammer
And almost got locked in the slammer,
But he was acquitted
For what he'd committed —
His lawyer had excellent grammar.

I wonder how the world appears through other people's eyes.
I wonder why this stranger laughs and why this other cries.
I wonder what the breath of life has whispered in their ears.
I wonder how they brave the day and reckon with the years.

I wonder what the others hope and fear and what they love.
I wonder how they see the world and what they make thereof.
I guess I can't be certain, but there *is* one thing I know:
If they don't worship at my church, they're gonna have to go.

You say you saw a dragonfly
And people say, "Congrats?"
But if you see a dragon fly,
Your belfry's checked for bats.

People get extremely tribal
On the topic of the Bible,
Making sure their son connects with
Someone who he genuflects with
To control who he has sects with.

I have found my solo hobby:
Eating ice cream with awareness,
Side-to-side, like Hammurabi,
Evening the top toward fairness
Till what's left is only bareness.

You cannot post a man as goods for sale.
His liberty, however,
Can be exchanged for monetary bail
When, unconvicted, he's confined to jail.
You never should say, "never."

Often had I wondered why I'd heard so many strangers
Claiming that no woman should become a politician.
Never could I fathom what could ever be the dangers,
So, to seek an answer, I consulted a logician.

After rigid reason had dismissed the incidental,
"Clearly," the logician said, "the issue's anatomic.
Never could a woman master matters governmental.
Female bids in pissing contests simply would be comic."

Oh, the time change is a-comin'
And you know it is a-bummin'
Me out.
Yes, I surely, sorely fear it
As each day's a-slippin' near it.
I'd shout
If I thought 'twould stop the shadders,
But it cain't and nothing matters.
Cain't cope.
I surrender me to darkness
Till the Marchtime comes to spark 'n us
Some hope.
But hope's a nope.
Cain't climb this slope.
No, the time change is a-comin'
And it really is a-bummin'
Me out.

I'm gastro-bathophobic, so
Please gracilely roll out the dough.
Chicago style should make me cry
And then defenestrate the pie.

But, otherwise, I care no wit
About what rests atop of it.
Fortuitism guides my choice
Select what's best and I'll rejoice.

Author's Note: The following are definitions of the fancy, obscure words in this poem:

- *Gastro-bathophobic*: afraid of deep food (a word I invented based on *gastro-* "stomach," *batho-* "depth," and *phob(os)* "fear").
- *Gracile*: thin.
- *Defenestrate*: to throw out a window.
- *Fortuitism*: the belief that natural events are driven by random chance.

I really want an ectomorph
— I'm less entranced by girls I dwarf —
Who's bathycolpian, for sure,
With callipygian allure.

But I'll find use for what's to hand,
Though she be stout and falsely tanned.
The only woman I can't want's
An unhygienic xanthodont.

Author's Note: The following are definitions of the fancy, obscure words in this poem:

- *Ectomorph*: a tall, thin person.
- *Bathycolpian*: deep-chested, having large breasts.
- *Callipygian*: having beautiful buttocks.
- *Xanthodont*: a person with yellow teeth.

An amorous man from Kentucky
Moved up to New York, feeling plucky.
His accent, however,
Just didn't sound clever.
And, so, he could never get lucky.

Fibonacci Verse

Fractalic,
Dactylic
Rhyming's euphonious,
Frenzied but also harmonious.
This Fibonacci-shaped poem intones mathematically.
Growth of the line length accelerates speedily, spelling the message out rather emphatically.
But, pretty quickly, as lines become longer and longer and longer and every new rhyme spreads out farther and farther and farther, the verse spins out crazily,
Leaving itself with a tortured, distended, and sprawling construction that hurries on faster and faster and faster through hustling metrically, costing the poetry what was predominant in the beginning: the triple rhyme, heard now but hazily.
This line just punctuates phrasally.

Author's Note: As the poem itself explains, the length, in metrical feet (dactyls here), of every line in this poem except the last one is determined by the Fibonacci sequence. The last line adds a sense of closure. There is end rhyme at the end of each line.

No one will ever encounter such suffering
As I endure when my movie is buffering.

He had always applauded equality,
But when rivalry weakened his wallet, he
Realigned his position:
He likes competition
But promotes a hierarchical polity.

The mystical master of Heaven
Declared, "Of the days, there'll be seven.
The one day to pester
Me on's when I rest.
Once at nine and again at eleven."

English poems should
Include some amplitude-some
Stress beats to be good.

It is also nice
For rhyming to match timing:
Endings that come twice

Sound superb to use,
Despite a fad to write a
Prose style in haikus.

An Englishman's haiku
Adapts to fit the language it
Is in. Now wouldn't you?

I didn't think I'd see your race
But stabbed my eyes out, just in case.

I love you truly, dear, I swear,
So please don't move away.
You see, the nanny's copper hair
Just accents the duvet.

Darling, you are the daytime and I am the night
And together we meet in the dawn.
We devote a few hours to commingling our light
And then I am silently gone.

Manhattan Cosmology

My child must pass New York my genes
When I have left this earth for Queens.
My grandkids then can pray me back
Along the Seven Subway Track
Which shuttles spirits to Manhattan.

But, if my child decides to leave,
My soul will never gain reprieve.
If, after I've departed, there's
No grandkid to perform the prayers,
Then I will surely ride to Staten
Island, past returning, on — oh! —
On the One-Way Verrazano.

Author's Note: The poems in this collection make fun of many different kinds of people. This poem makes fun of me and other people from Manhattan, New York City. Many New Yorkers, whether from Manhattan or other parts of New York City, are very proud of New York and often fall prey to feeling like there is nothing beyond the city limits. Manhattanites, however, are often even more extreme, succumbing to the attitude that Manhattan alone is the entire world and that even the other boroughs of New York City lie beyond reality. This phenomenon is a product of the worldwide tendency of city-dwellers to feel pride in their cities and the tendency of Americans to be proud of the exact location they live in. New York is a city in America, so its residents are subject to a double dose of pride.

(Train Announcer:)
The next stop is Grand Central — 42nd Street.

(Train:)
GLANG! EEEEKH, EEEEKH, BREEKH! GRMMM, GRMMM, GRMMMMM...

(Man:)
Yo, my dudes! Over here. Listen: birds aren't real
And the earth is as flat as my abs.
No, legit. I'm as ripped as this shirt. Take a feel.
I've been doing my exercise dabs.
Like my face in my elbow, my hand to the sky,
To the sky with the birds — that's the drones.
Hey, did you know the pyramids want us to die
To replace us with Jesus's clones?
There's this Book of the Dead. Of the dead! Swear to God.
And the Ghost, God, and Jesus makes three.
Plus I had some old cousins — were triplets — shit's odd.
That's the Trinity, triad, y'see?
'Cause the triads are China dudes, all Yin and Yang.
That shit's balance, like gymnasts, y'know?
Yo! You seen the Olympics? That's Greek and, like, dang!
On TV, that shit. Hell of a show!
And, think: shows — they're on Broadway. That's Jews and it's gays
And it's tourists and rich people, too.
Corporations are rich people. Corporate pays
All the workers, the poor. That's just true.
And what's true is that bird drones are watching our lives
And they know all the words that we say.
Hide your children, your daughters, your fish, and your wives
And then bow at the heavens and pray.

'Cause the government's Jesus funds all of the birds
And a Jesus is made from a fish —
That's a fish that gets paid well and knows all the words
To respond to a prayer — that's a wish.

(Train Announcer:)
We apologize that we are briefly delayed.
There's a passenger sick deep in Queens.

(Man:)
Man it's everyone! People and fish both get paid!
And, like, shit! Can't you see what that means?
It means money is power and ill-gotten gains
And, think: knowledge is power, as well,
So then money is sickness that's got in our brains
And they shouldn't have taught us to spell.
It's in thinking and nowhere is safe anymore.
It's a swarm, like fake birds, but it's men.

(Train Announcer:)
The delay is resolved. We were told to ignore
All of Queens. We're now moving again.

(Man:)
I mean, everyone's in on it. Fuck! You and me!
It's existence and damn! Oh my God!
And the Ghost, God, and Jesus — that — whoah! — that makes three.
Plus my cousins were triplets — shit's odd.
And, like, triplets is trinity, triads, y'see?
We got China dudes, all Yin and Yang.
It's all balance like gymnasts. We're all gonna be —
Here's what's up: —

(Train:)

GRMMM, GRMMM, BREEKH! EEEEKH, EEEEKH, GLANG!

(Train Announcer:)
This stop is Grand Central — 42nd Street.

Deciphering this prophecy
Requires a special phonic key.
The meaning lies behind the guise
Of rhymed but nonsense poetry.

The obstruents and nasals hop
One place (except the glottals). Swap
Most vowels, too, to somewhere new:
They turn by length and then they stop.

Core vowels, glides, and liquids, though,
And diphthongs keep their status quo.
Just make the shifts and then your gift's
The wisdom in the verse below:

Vuh thalzher uhzh vuth krashuhthoo,
Howizher harrs vayr lishe ngee goo
Wull shimbe reloosh shruhng immoo droosh
Shruhng mamthimth vep'th lundwuthputoo.

Author's Note: If you follow the instructions in the first three stanzas of this poem and decipher the last stanza (which requires some knowledge of linguistics), you should end up with the following prophecy as the last stanza:

The solver of this prophecy,
However harsh their life may be
Will find relief from any grief
From nonsense that's linguisticky.

Quite often in a yesteryear,
I'd ponder over life.
Like would I lead a grand career
Or even win a wife?

But now I stare down new concerns,
Through crusted, heavy lids
Like what's the deal with tax returns
And do I hate my kids?

Before I followed trends,
The kids at school said, "You're not cool,"
But now they're all my friends.

Soon after my goy chick
Had birthed our new boychik,
We argued with heated responses.

My wife's mind was closed to
What Jews are supposed to
Have done to their baby boys' schwanzes.

So I got dynamic
And I Abrahamically
Pled for our child's circumcision.

But she is a Hindu.
That's not what her kin do.
Our faiths were approaching collision.

She questioned why God would
Insist Jews have odd wood,
But I said that loss comes with Shiva.

"The cut is a trigger
To make it grow bigger."
With that, she was whetting the cleaver.

Modern Dance

I groove alone to tunes in my garage:
I sway and clap and pantomime frottage.
I pump my fists and dent the stagnant air
And buffet buttocks that were never there.
And then I shift my shoulders back to front.
God, what ever happened to dancing?

Since history won't long recall
The deed they did and why,
We raise this two-by-four-foot wall
To puzzle passersby.

On, Comet! on, Cupid! on, Donner and Blitzen!
We're skipping the house that depraved little shit's in.

Since he, of late, was home all day,
"He's really very rude," they'd say.
"And likely lies a-bed.
He never brings a game to play
Or even knocks to just say, 'Hey.'
I kind of wish he'd move away."
The fact is, he was dead.

Don't you dare say I don't matter!
I'm the greatest, maybe batter!
Whoops. No. "Better." Missed the spelling.
Guess I'm sloppy when I'm yelling.
Never mind.

Have you seen my evil henchman?
Not the eyepatched German sniper.
Not the curly-mustached Frenchman.
Not the titan. Not the sprite and
Not the "ethnic" with the viper.

This one's handsome. U. S. accent.
Prying. Useless. Tends to hover.
Failed to get a crucial fax sent...
Wait. Don't sweat it. Now I get it:
He's the good guy undercover.

One Rich Man to Another

My friend, you cannot trust the proletariat.
What kind of psychos let you treat them like they're shit?

How fortunate that God bestowed the planet onto us.
You'd almost think we made him up to do exactly thus.

Blessed Jacob's son Joseph was sold into slave'ry.
He wasn't a slave, but his brothers still sold 'im.
That trick was despicable, criminal knave'ry
As some kind of lawyer should prob'ly have told 'em.
Eleven to one though's a son of a gun. Though
The laws declare one thing, it's folks must uphold 'em
'Cause God doesn't do much to scold 'em.

In the bid to rebuild the smashed egg-man that day,
Tell me, what was the role for king's *horses* to play?

Never trust an ugly stranger.
Hot ones, though, are worth the danger.

If God will purge the whole of earth for omnipresent sin,
Then that means that stupidity is virtuously in.

On the Seventh Day

You know it would please us
To honor Lord Jesus,
But folks can't just give up their Sundays.
'Cause Monday's for working
And Friday's for shirking
And weekends are coming undone days.

Since church is more taxing
Than simply relaxing,
We can't come to praise God's perfection.
Like Jesus before us,
An end must restore us
And grant us our own resurrection.
But no one can sit in our section!

A gallant who visited France a lot
Used to get in his lord's lady's pants a lot.
Both his shield and his sword
He employed when he warred,
But, in private, he worked with his Lancelot.

I wouldn't be a prostitute if something paid me better,
Like you, sir, 'd be with someone else, if you could really get 'er.

Christ, while Lord, is also savior.
This is quite distinct behavior.
Typically, a savior'd save us
From a lord who would enslave us.
He works too much.

Oh, wherefore art thou Romeo?
I wish you was my homie, yo.
As I could wed a Capulet,
But daddy ain't gon' let me get
Me coupled with a Montague.
Boy, why you ain't some brother who
My father would esteem it good
For me to marry? God, wish you
Derived from my side of the hood.
Oh, would instead, my love, thy name were "Boo."

My son came home from school one day
And said he now could read
And I was stricken with dismay —
I knew where *that* could lead:

He might read books and learn the world
I'd left him wasn't great,
That life was not perfection, and
That people had to work
To fight the looming pain that swirled
Around him and that hate
Was everywhere, in every land —
A *good* man couldn't shirk

The moral obligation of
Promoting empathy and love,
The duty I'd ignored.
I paused before I thought to say,
"You know the pen, son, 's pretty gay.
You ought to try the sword.

"See: thought is for the weak, my boy.
Use force to get ahead
'Cause only power brings true joy."
Then nothing more was said.

And giving that advice was wise:
I'm still a hero in his eyes.

A song that's sung to sing the song you sing so it is sung.
A song with that as lyrics, though, is murder on the tongue.

Perpetuation

Society's a construct made
Of all the things we say are true
And it's a place of turpitude,
Corrupt and evil, through and through.
Or so my friends all tell me and,
I wouldn't dare not take their cue,
So now I feel obliged to pass
This sacred wisdom on to you
So you can spread the evil too.

Police Report, or A Night before Morning

'Twas a night before morning, when all through the house
All the windows were open. My beautiful spouse
Was away on some business, and so she could not
Be disturbed by the breezes, and, man, was it hot.
At a quarter to midnight, I lay in my bed
With the slowness of slumber beginning to spread
From the roof of my brain to the floors of my toes.
I was *this* close to dreaming of columns and rows
When a skid and a crash and a honk in the distance
Invaded my ears and announced the existence
Of a problem that somebody needed to solve.
But I thought to myself, *it'll prob'ly resolve*
And be fixed by the morning, as sleep-slipping men
Often do when it's midnight (well, nearly). But then,
From the kitchen, there came a percussive assault
On my ears. I awoke. *You must find who's at fault*,
Said a voice in my skull that arose from the deep
When I woke into ninety degrees from my sleep.
It was probably rage and it wanted the blood
Of the villain who'd shattered my peace, so I thud-
ed downstairs to the kitchen, perspiring and spitting
And found there a dwarf with a peg leg just sitting
In a chair by the window. His purple-like tux
Was a size or two larger than he was. "Deluxe!"
He exclaimed as I swung in the room like a switch.
I was flailing a shoe by the lace when, "My pitch!"
Cried the dwarf as he hurdled himself from his seat
And his leg and his peg with a turbulent beat
On the porcelain flooring went *thumpety-clack.*
"I'll deliver my pitch to the gentleman: Black
Is the midnight" — He gestured about — "and the moon
Is a glimmering cluster of salt. Opportun-

ities gather for secrets and starlight and sprites
To converge on the moment, for marvelous sights
To be witnessed by mortals who'd never believe,
If my master, René, didn't help them perceive!"
While exclaiming, "perceive," in a bravely dramatic
But unpromising tone that was blankly emphatic,
The mysterious dwarf, with his purple-like sleeves
And the gusto of gusts in the dead autumn leaves,
Waved his arms at the window he stood just beside
Which like each of the others was open as wide
As its frame would allow. With a groan and a shuffle,
Through the window there slithered a man with a ruffle
On his collar and each of his wrist-sleeves. The shirt
Had been white but, at present, was sullied with dirt
And with blood from the numerous wounds in his gut
That were crowded with fragments of metal that jut-
Ted like shelves. It was clear that this stranger had wrecked
And destroyed both his car and his gut. I'd neglect-
Ted to answer the call of the crash. Now the crash
Had come calling. The man tried to stand but a gash
In his stomach prevented his rise, so he twisted
On the tiles and he struggled until he desisted.
Then the dwarf flapped his purple-like sleeves at the gore.
"The Fantastic René will now bleed on your floor."

I've never worn a gargling stole
Nor heard an "I'm indoors!" bell
Nor eaten at a Cows in Pics
Nor smelled a plant called s'moresbell.

I've never held a swargling pole
Nor only-tell-a-lie phone.
But, then, in just Two Thousand Six,
I'd never seen an iPhone.

Think: Ownership confuses life.
At first, it's just, "I own this knife
And, if it's sitting on a stone,
Then there it stays. It's left alone."

But soon it isn't just a knife.
I have and hold my land and wife.
And, if a man has weapons, he
Can own my stuff by owning me.

And slavery's not where it ends.
Quite soon, you'll have to purchase friends.
Eventually, to man's disgrace,
We'll start appraising time and space.

So don't assume that you can own
Just anything. Mankind is prone
To run with things till reason dies.
It's safest just to share your fries.

My favorite white whine's a good
"There goes the neighborhood."

Men must be taller than women
If they have intention to date them
And this is a lot more important
Than whether they secretly hate them
Or plan to routinely berate them
And, so, many quarrels await them.

Pride

They tell me I was born stark nude,
But I would never act so lewd
And let folks take a gander,
So I have filed a suit and sued
My parents for their slander.

How curious that everyone who seeks the master race
Unearths themselves and not some strangers in another place.

The populace will simply not revere
An ugly or an average man, I fear,
Which means, considering the praise he got,
The Savior Jesus Christ was super hot.
QED

It's time to get rid of the planet.
It's flawed, so I say that we ban it.

I don't exactly hate you.
It's just that you're the worst.
I know that I berate you,
But I have never cursed.

You should know that you're a lame-o
If you're saying "No problemo."
If you otherwise speak gringo,
Stick to using gringo lingo.
Or, if you're intent to borrow,
Borrow like there's no tomorrow.
Take each word and phrase from Spanish
Till you've seen the stockpile vanish.
For they say on Easter Island,
Where they've borrowed for a while and
Taken Lunes through Domingo,
"Do it. It takes tú to tingo."

Tingo (Pascuense, Easter Island): to take all the objects one desires from the house of a friend, one at a time, by borrowing them.

    - *The Meaning of Tingo*, Adam Jacot de Boinod

Do not despond when life seems overmuch to bear.
You cannot doubt the world is firmly on your side,
As proof of this is clear. Think: otherwise, from where
Is all that weight compressing out your breath supplied?

It is not how they read it. It's how it is said. Don't depend upon cues on the paper. Embed all your rhythm and rhyming in language, not ink. While a line break's convenient, it's not how you think when you utter a sentence. It falsifies flow. When your readers speak meter, they simply should know.

A homophobic black man and a racist who was gay
Fell naturally to arguing upon a dreary day.
Progressive Becky got involved but soon became distressed:
She couldn't find a side to pick since both were quite oppressed.
And, so, she wept and each man crept quite cautiously away.

Hunting innovative synergistic management solutions,
Corporate reads the Vedics, Taoists, Buddhists, and Confucians.

Love's always fruitless. I won't be a dope again.
Wait. There's a woman. I'm flooded with hope again.

His "I love you," 's really hollow
If he doesn't like and follow.

That so-and-so are people too's
An old idea — nothing new —
But, somehow, we're so into it,
We keep returning to that shit.

At first, I thought it was a hat
And placed it on my head.
But then I put it on my foot
And it's a shoe instead!

Bear in mind this powerful mnemonic:
"No. That's not the way to use 'ironic.'
Yes. I'm overusing 'It's iconic.'
No. Your cough is not, in fact, bubonic.
Yes. That creepy symbol is Masonic."
And there can't be doubt that it is true that,
"Since you're asking, this is not platonic."
Absolutely never misconstrue that
Most important, most delusive last one
Since it's often known to pull a fast one.

Scat Sonnet

Shebeep sheboop skwedeet skwedeet skwedoo.
Shebwoop shebweep skedleedla skeedla dwop.
Dwedow deshoop despleet desheedel shoo.
Debeedum dow dewop dewopwa shpop.
Lepwoipli poitel pow. Lesklip leskleek.
Leplack lepleddel plop. Lepluddel plap.
Freskappedett freskett freskett leteek.
Feretta tlap tefrapla tackla klap.
Wesplow wepring wespengla spengla pree.
Webambla blambla dappla dippla dow.
Uh yeewa yeewa wooyih wooyih wee.
Wewaawa yaawa yaawa waia wow.
Jeskeepit kleep. Dejeepit dadgit dloe.
Jegow jedrow jeskow jejibb. Let's go!

Author's Note: This poem demonstrates that the rhythm of a metrical, rhyming poem (in this case a Shakespearean sonnet) can exist without words that mean anything. Personally, I think it's best to give attention to both form *and* meaning, but few people choose to only put effort into form while many people focus on meaning, so I think this poem is a fun departure from the norm. In the spirit of interest in form, all the nonsense sounds are chosen carefully in order to create detailed patterns that go beyond just the basic sonnet structure. Ultimately, though, this poem is more of an absurdity than a witticism.

Think: The speed of sight
Is the speed of flight —
It's the speed of flight
Of the flight of light.
And the speed of light
Is the speed of white.
That's because, in sight,
Gathered light is white.
So the flight of light
Is the flight of white,
Which is the creation of the suburbs.

I need some new glasses
To survey nice asses
Without an abundance of starin'.

My vision's too blurry
To scan in a hurry
With those that I'm currently wearin'.

It's hard to glean data
On which women matta
With strangers all glarin' at present.

Unwanted attention
Is gettin' me clenchin'
My muscles. It's kinda unpleasant.

Shakespeare Excuses His Infidelity

But wherefore wouldst, fair maid, that I should go?
I stray in but that I do sharply ache
From love more deep than man hath bravèd ere.

Departing from tradition is to grow.
I stray from custom. *Thee* I'd ne'er forsake.
If I all women love, how bold and rare!

More fortune be with thee if I bestow
On thee so strong a love that all partake.
If good attend capacity to care,
Reproach me not for having love to spare.

Remove your shoes
When you come in.
The avenues
That you have been
Out walking on
Are caked in grime.
Who knows what's gone
And spread its slime
On everything?
Just Saturday,
A guy was flinging
Sludge away.
I witnessed this
While going piss.

Remove your shoes, my friend,
When entering the house.
We don't want to offend
My (fussy) — lovely! — spouse.
Your shoes might track that scat
That settles from the air.
He's quite opposed to that
Inside beyond this stair.
He works himself to bones.
Can't come back home to stains.
That company he owns
Demands such work and pains.
It's not a simple goal,
Producing steam from coal.

Anything printed in typeface is accurate.
Web forums say you're the problem? Then, smack! You're it.

I'm trying to be just like you.
Stop trying to be me.
If we don't pause to think this through,
I'm not sure who we'll be.

I crept a narrow alley close to dark.
The light was wanting, so I often felt
My way along the street I could not mark.
To circumvent detection, oft I knelt.
For failure to escape would cost my head,
So silence was the comrade on whose skill
I most depended as I plied my tread,
Lest thump betray me and my doom fulfill.
And so I slunk in hushed penumbral cloak
Escaping from the alley's steering chute,
Then sought concealment underneath an oak.
I sprinted to the tree, but kicked a root.
"Oh fucking shit godammit Jesus ooh!"
Then I was fine again... but murdered too.

Mister Green with the rope in the hall!
What?! I'm wrong?! I will murder you all
With — the card's the lead pipe...
Who still builds with that type?
Just a second. I'll smash in the wall.

Meseems my lance attacks be woeful weak,
But this my blade assurèd's nigh OP.
A spammèd sword is then the fit technique
Wherewith to own my foe and victory
And thus the lord of PvP to be.

In a country that's waging a war
That is focused on fighting the poor,
It's a little bit strange
That each policy change
Grows the number of poor even more.

The men who mugged my dad
Let slip a swear in the affair
And *that* he said was bad.

That Spy Life (A Rap by Benjamoney Coinicott Cashavitz)

(Yelled by way of obligatory introduction:)
It's 'Jamoney!

(Rapped:)
Yo, I be spittin' mad rhymes
'Bout committin' mad crimes
And committin' them crimes
On the government dime.
The CIA is my employer.
I'm a government-funded undercover warrior.
I perpetrate me them clandestine acts
And stop me some them terrorist attacks.
People gripin' 'bout how I do torture.
I don't know. I just be foll'win' orders.
Is it wrong to be a waterboarder?

(Sung:)
I be spyin'.
I be lyin'.
All the people always cryin'
That I'm evil,
Say I'm raidin',
Straight invadin',
In they lives, but I'm just aidin'
In retrieval
Of some knowledge,
Data trawlage,
Like I'm workin' in a college,
Paper writin'.
People holl'rin',

But I'm schol'rin'
In a field I'm straight a ball'r in:
Evil fightin'.

(Rapped:)
I be droppin' mad lines
Like I'm fishin' that brine
And I'm droppin' them lines
'Bout how I'm straight a spy.
The NSA is who I work for.
I'm a government-sponsored secret shadow lurker.
I follow people from behind they backs
And bug they homes to gather all the facts.
People mad I went and filmed them naked,
But we might need that if the terr'rists take them.
Calm down, y'all. It ain't like rights are sacred.

(Sung:)
I be spyin'.
I be lyin'.
All the people always cryin'
That I'm evil,
Say I'm raidin',
Straight invadin',
In they lives, but I'm just aidin'
In retrieval
Of some knowledge,
Data trawlage,
Like I'm workin' in a college,
Paper writin'.
People holl'rin',
But I'm schol'rin'
In a field I'm straight a ball'r in:
Evil fightin'.

(Rapped:)
I never made it to South Amer'ca.
I would've, though, 'f i'd been another era.
As it is, I fight the War on Terror.
I know the cap'tal of every country,
But not for school. I'm just 'a put it bluntly:
A coup d'état might need to start abruptly.
I got the fliest of occupations.
What I do is secret, but it saves the nation.
They hardly ever launch investigations.

(Rapped:)
I be bustin' mad bars
Like they never check cards
But I read all them cards
For the stripes and the stars.
The DNI's my one superior.
Every one of my motives straight-up mad ulterior.
I'm deep involved in every op that's black.
I, on the daily, launch a cyb'r attack.
People pissed I Trojan Horsed 10 Downin'.
But what you thinkin'? That we out here clownin'?
We gon' know you. Who care where your town in?

(Sung:)
I be spyin'.
I be lyin'.
All the people always cryin'
That I'm evil,
Say I'm raidin',
Straight invadin',
In they lives, but I'm just aidin'
In retrieval

Of some knowledge,
Data trawlage,
Like I'm workin' in a college,
Paper writin'.
People holl'rin',
But I'm schol'rin'
In a field I'm straight a ball'r in:
Evil fightin'.

Australians have feelings too.
I learned that watching Mythic Quest.
I probably already knew,
But television is the best.

The Charmer

He's never met a woman that he didn't like down deep.
It could be he's a feminist. He's probably a creep.

The Convert

"Uh, Professor, I don't get it,
Why do people choose to read that?
Does it just not fit my taste?"

She said, "If you really let it,
This will sway you. You'll concede that
This has moved your very soul."

So I dug and mined each sentence,
But I simply couldn't strike it,
Strike the value that I chased.

But, in class, in deep repentance,
I was told just why I like it,
Word for word, and now I'm whole.

Medieval times had ended and the Renaissance was through
When man achieved Enlightenment and looked on life anew
And everyone was certain of the proper things to do.
Improvement governs gentlemen.

Henri had eyed Lucien's old mistress, so they set for dawn
A rendezvous with pistols and their seconds on the lawn,
For dueling is more dignified than proletary brawn.
Sound reason governs gentlemen.

Lucien arrived at half past four and waited for Henri.
He'd brought, as second, Antoine, quite the heir to pedigree.
Young Antoine'd brought the pistols, leaving all as it should be.
Fit manners govern gentlemen.

Henri was there at ten to five but came without Pierre,
The second who, with Antoine, 'd set the duel for then and there.
Lucien deplored this absence for delaying the affair.
Wise judgment governs gentlemen.

Henri was not alone, however, as he'd brought along
An Afric youth whose wish to leave was evident and strong.
For slavery was legal then and therefore wasn't wrong.
Good morals govern gentlemen.

"Let's start!" Henri declared at once without a greeting first,
Which shook Lucien and Antoine who were solemnly immersed
In waiting on Pierre with ire that later could be nursed.
Harsh grudges govern gentlemen.

"But where's Pierre?" Lucien inquired. "Our seconds must be here

Officiating over us, or else it would appear
That we had fought like savages, unplanned and cavalier."
Keen forethought governs gentlemen.

Henri replied, "Pierre cannot be present here this morn
But Andre here" — he gestured to his slave — "was simply born
To second me in anything." (Young Andre looked forlorn.)
Preparedness governs gentlemen.

"You see, Pierre is busy with some dueling of his own:
Francois implied he's English by extending him a scone,
A slight for which two pistols now are needed to atone."
Fair balance governs gentlemen.

"In fact, Pierre is dueling with Francois just over there.
Behind those trees, I'd speculate, they're holding the affair.
But, come, let's start, ourselves. I think it's time that we prepare."
Swift promptness governs gentlemen.

"Outrageous!" cried Lucien. "A slave as Antoine's counterpart
Insults good Antoine, stabbing through his honor to the heart.
Henri replied, "What other choice is there? I say we start."
Pragmatics governs gentlemen.

Lucien just gaped aghast at the perversion of his plan,
So Andre offered boldly to seek out a nobler man
To second, but Henri said he'd be late although he ran.
Awareness governs gentlemen.

Lucien continued gaping till keen Antoine spoke the fact
That dueling was illegal and to loiter would attract
The guard at such an hour, so 'twas time that they transact.
Astuteness governs gentlemen.

Accepting Antoine's guidance, proud Lucien deigned to relent:
"What is must be," he muttered, "so it's time for the event."
The duelists took from Antoine each a matching armament.
Just fairness governs gentlemen.

"As custom holds, each pistol is a smooth bore," Antoine said
"And bears no graven rifling to direct the flying lead.
To aim is hardly possible, so none should wind up dead."
Wise safety governs gentlemen.

On hearing none should die, blanched Andre grew more halely swart.
"I do not need a murder for the guardsmen to distort
And pin on poor black Andre," thought the slave who'd witnessed court.
Evasion governs gentlemen.

"As custom dictates," Antoine said, "the slave and I must plead,
With each of you — Lucien, Henri — to set aside the deed
You came intent to carry out, so peace may intercede."
Persuasion governs gentlemen.

Keen Andre started right away: "Monsieur Henri," he said,
"Refraining from this pistol fight ensures that none fall dead."
Henri was moved: "Lucien, let's quit and put this all to bed."
Good counsel governs gentlemen.

Lucien became incensed, however: "I shall never heed
The guidance of an underling nor man of Afric breed.
My honor now is triply mocked. Prepare to brave the deed!"
Bold umbrage governs gentlemen.

Though Antoine wished to try his tongue, the time had clearly passed.
Lucien was undissuadable. The duel must start at last.
Sighed Antoine, "Load in powder and one leaden pyroclast."
Acceptance governs gentlemen.

The duelists readied then their guns and Antoine cried commands:
"Ten paces each, then each must turn exactly where he stands."
The gunmen took their places. Then they raised their pistoled hands.
Procedure governs gentlemen.

"Now cock your weapons," Antoine called. The duelists did as told
While Andre prayed to Heaven for the chance to yet behold
A future past a week from now, despite what might unfold.
Blind faith must govern gentlemen.

"You fire on three," cried Antoine and the gunmen's gazes met.
Each stare was steel till "Un!" was called and palms began to sweat.
When "Deux!" appeared, all eyes were closed and muscles tensely set.
Reactions govern gentlemen.

But just before the stroke of "Trois!", though ready as could be,
Lucien began exclaiming "Wait!" and so too did Henri,
As each desired to live his life instead of risk a three.
Reflection governs gentlemen.

Brave Andre dared to feel relief and hope they'd met an end.
"Oh, thank you, Heaven," Andre thought. "I knew I could depend
Upon your gracious providence for those who would ascend."
Shared gods must govern gentlemen.

And all was calm for half a breath until a starting bang
Resounded through the dawning sky and suddenly there rang
A shriek of pain from paused Henri who clutched a mortal pang.
Endurance governs gentlemen.

Henri was shot within his gut, but not by proud Lucien:
Pierre, Henri's old second had just missed his own foe then,
Beyond the trees while dueling as his partner'd called out "When!"

Obeisance governs gentlemen.

Henri, believing stalled Lucien had fired the mortal shot,
Compressed his slipping trigger, hoping lead would bring to rot
The traitor who had killed him, but he struck an oaken knot.
Reprisal governs gentlemen.

Unscathed Lucien, when fired upon, reacted with his gun,
But smooth bores miss all targets and the leaden load, unspun,
Reflected off a stone toward near the place it had begun.
Essaying governs gentlemen.

Lucien was spared but Antoine screamed. The latter had been struck
By that which true Lucien had loosed with righteousness and pluck.
A shame it now seemed Antoine was a man of evil luck.
God's fortune governs gentlemen.

For just a moment, silence reigned, once Antoine had succumbed,
But soon poor Andre's whimpering could not remain bedumbed
By shock and soon his pacing sounded vehemently drummed.
Transition governs gentlemen.

Lucien surveyed the scene about and saw Henri deceased.
The pistol which Henri still clutched would bring *him* blame, at least.
But Antoine's corpse was weaponless; suspicion'd be increased.
Appraisals govern gentlemen.

And, worst of all, the Afric slave was witness to the crimes
And might endanger just Lucien by dropping guards some dimes.
Oh, woe then was Lucien he'd triggered one too many times.
Compunction governs gentlemen.

While sliding down his pistol into Antoine's slackened grip

To set a self-explaining scene, Lucien did not let slip
The gaze he'd trained on Andre and each who-knew-how-loose lip.
Attention governs gentlemen.

Wise Andre's mouth was used to scornful glares from thin-lipped whites,
But this was clearly different, like when someone flies or fights,
So Andre turned and faced Lucien to keep him in his sights.
Discernment governs gentlemen.

"The guard will be upon us any moment, noble lord,"
Quick Andre blurted desperately. "It's time to quit the sward."
He held but little hope, though, as a slave is oft ignored.
The gentle govern gentlemen.

Quite motionless, Lucien assessed his options in a trance.
He could not leave a witness living anywhere in France.
But, weaponless and foppish, he had one remaining chance.
Nonviolence governs gentlemen.

"Boy, sable slave, come hither. I shall forge the fiscal path
For you to sail to England, so you'll never face the wrath
Of guilt-assigning guardsmen. Think: you're not a slave in Bath."
Largesse must govern gentlemen.

Lucien concluded speaking, so mild Andre dared a turn:
"My lord, a gift so generous I surely cannot spurn."
"Fantastic!" cried Lucien. "So, till interment, we adjourn!"
Decorum governs gentlemen.

Lucien and Andre quit the scene a minute's tick before
The guard arrived and found whose deaths bestrewed the meadow's floor.
It seemed Henri and Antoine'd settled up and tied a score.
Brave stances govern gentlemen.

The guardsmen thought Henri and Antoine'd shot each other dead,
But then they noticed, in an oaken knot, some extra lead,
Which might've meant another party'd feuded, fired, and fled.
Detection governs gentlemen.

But nothing could be known for sure, as every other tree
Exhibited a bullet scar from duelists firing free
On this or that preceding dawn. A court would be at sea.
Routines must govern gentlemen.

So, thus, Lucien's embattled honor met a settled peace.
Henri, the bold aggressor, 's threat had brought itself to cease.
Renown defended, just Lucien could proudly flee to Nice.
Fair outcomes govern gentlemen.

Behold then how awakenings reveal to man what's right.
Enlightenment and progress always shed a perfect light
That proffers all humanity discriminating sight.
Believe and you're a gentleman.

To fight for what's right is the worthiest action
That ever can be undertaken.
A shame, then, it is that what's right is a factional
Notion that might be mistaken.

We must support the EPA. It's plain for all to see:
If we had no environment, then where'd we even be?

A cumulonimbus comes floating
While captain and mate are out boating.
The following cloudburst
Drowns Cap with a loud burst:
The nautical form of promoting.

Now, Jesus loves me. This I know
Because the Bible tells me so.
But that's as far as things can go.
I'm not gay, Christ. No hugging, Bro.

If life's a simulation
With logic-circuit rules,
Then praying for salvation's
To ask for hacking tools.

A magic wizard in the sky
Is unconvincing as a lie
And so he must be truth.

The scholars first proclaimed that melanin was sin.
They later faced about and called it magic.
Perhaps, if they just claimed that it was melanin,
Then humankind's affairs would be less tragic.

The Origin of [PLURAL NOUN]: A Fill-in-the-Blanks Sonnet

The history of all the [PLURAL NOUN]
Began when [NAME], in [NUMBER] BCE,
Observed the [NOUN] that [VERB]-ed in his/her town
Was much too [ADJECTIVE] for it to be
Of any use to [PLURAL NOUN] at all
And [ADVERB] started [VERB]-ing day and night
Until, when [NUMBER] months had passed and Fall
Was near and need for [NOUN] was at its height,
The useless [NOUN] was taken out to [VERB]
The situation and it [VERB]-ed too much!
Then, [NOUN] was lost, till [NAME] came to disturb
The fearful silence: "[EXCLAMATION]! Touch
The [NOUN] with these. They're [PLURAL NOUN]. We'll live!"
The people did and things were [ADJECTIVE].

In days of old
When knights were bold
And Venmo wasn't invented,
They tipped their bards
With credit cards
And walked away contented.

If you care about balance, you're happy to learn
Of a college curriculum structured to spurn
The traditional focus on writings by white
Men and shed on perspectives from others some light.

But the real thing that's shrinking the role of the DWEM
In our schooling's the switching from English to STEM,
So, while white men no longer command the whole scene,
Their successor's a colorless, sexless machine.

Author's Note: "DWEM" is a term that was popular among social justice activists in the 1990s. It is short for "dead white European male." "STEM" is a common abbreviation of "science, technology, engineering, and mathematics," something you probably already know since people still use the term.

If brevity's the soul of wit,
This quip is done. Full stop. That's it.

The speaker felt quite proud.
Despite a lack of proper facts,
He'd spoken very loud.

I studied engineering, so I'm now a philistine.
My sister studied English. She is one of many Luddites.
She thinks that plastic bags cause climate change, that those align
And I know nothing fancy. Don't read novels. Don't eat crudités.

Author's Note: "The Two Cultures and the Scientific Revolution" is a speech that was given by C. P. Snow in 1959. Snow was a novelist, but his academic training was in chemistry and physics and his speech laments his observation that people who were familiar with both science and literature had become rare by his time because of academic specialization and the rise of a major rift between the culture of science and the culture of what he calls "the literary intellectuals." A transcript of the speech has been published in a short volume and it's a very interesting read. Highly recommend.

We arrived at a town so homogenous
That the folks on the sidewalk kept dodgin' us.
We were skirted like trash
Till we brandished our cash
And they eagerly set about lodgin' us.

The Urse: A Complaint

While what a dog is to a wolf, an urse is to a bear,
No ancient people bred the urse, which I think isn't fair.
I thought of it, so it should be.
Why won't the world consider me?
It's like my thousand times great grandpa didn't even care.

Thoreauly Disappointing
(On Henry David Thoreau's "My Life Has Been the Poem I Would Have Writ")

My life has been the poem I would have writ,
But I could not both live and utter it.
That's for the best. My mind's devoid of wit.
There's no one who would want to hear that shit.

Author's Note: The first two lines of this poem are the entirety of Henry David Thoreau's poem "My Life Has Been the Poem I Would Have Writ" verbatim. The other two lines are my addition.

Christ is said to value mercy
And to govern all creation.
This has stirred some controversy:
Why is there such tribulation?
Are we ailing 'cause he's failing?
No. He's simply on vacation.
When he chooses to be finished,
All our pain will be diminished.

Sure, Muslims pray on special rugs
And Jews require that hat.
But Christians act out drinking blood
And no one questions that.

Women rear the children while the men go die in battle.
Basically, all young adults must serve the role of cattle.
Dairy is the yield for which you feed and house a daughter,
While a son is muscle to be ushered to the slaughter.
And some people really like that system.

For now *two thousand* years, there have just, at the most,
Been three persons of God we can thank
For our blessings: the Father, the Son, and the Ghost.
But, today, we release a fourth: Hank!

Vernal Equinox

Germans call this season "frühling."
Spaniards name it "primavera."
Welshmen say the term is "gwanwyn."
Shetland trawlers go with "voar," so

Let's resolve this with a rüling:
It is "springtime" in this era.
Let the Anglophonic man win.
Some speak Spanish — English more so.
Till that changes.

We named our daughter Charity
And so she hoards her wealth.
We named our second daughter Hope
And so she forecasts doom.
We named the third girl Temperance.
She's drunk away her health.
We named the fourth one Mercy and
It's worse than you assume.
So, after thinking hard and long
About what all'd been going wrong,
We named the last Rebellion
And she has zero clue
Of what to try to do.

Vitamin D

Darker skin needs more extensive outdoor sun exposure.
White skin's better suited to a prison-style enclosure.
We're doing racism wrong.

LEVITIES BEYOND ENGLISH

Author's Note: The following are some attempts at humorous verse in languages other than English with English translations. Each poem is supposed to be metrical and rhyme in its original language. Any weaknesses in style or content are, as always, my responsibility, especially since my speaking ability in the languages used in these poems is much weaker than my English ability.

Hermanos (Spanish)
Mi hermano se llama Sansón
Y no es un Juan o Ramón.
Compartimos un padre,
También una madre,
Pero *yo* no soy siempre cabrón.

(*Brothers*
My brother's name is Sansón
And he isn't a Juan or Ramón.
We share a father
And also a mother,
But *I* am not an asshole all the time.)

* * *

Poema a una Foto (Spanish)
Creo que te amo pero no estoy seguro.
¿Cómo se puede saber?
¡Ai! ¡Qué loco cuando no nos hemos encontrado!
¿Qué puede un hombre hacer?
Oi. Me supongo beber.

(*Poem to a Photo*
I think I love you but I'm not sure.
How can one know?

Ah! How crazy when we haven't met!
What can a man do?
Ugh. I guess drink.)

* * *

Mauvais Amis (French)
Je pense que j'ai besoin de plus amis
Car ceux que j'ai
Ne disent jamais
Qu'ils m'aiment. Ils m'évitent tous les jours aussi.
Je simplement
Mens tout le temps.
Mon style c'est différent. C'est qui je suis.
Un homme doit être soi. Pense: c'est la vie.

(*Bad Friends*
I think I need more friends
Because the ones I have
Never say
That they like me. They also avoid me every day.
I just
Lie all the time.
My style is different. It's who I am.
A man must be himself. Think: that's life.)

* * *

Katzenunfug (German)
Meine Katze ist sehr artig.
Meine Katze ist sehr süß.
Meine Katze ist — Ach! Wart! Ich
Muß das reparieren. Tschüss.

(*Cat Mischief*

159

My cat is very well-behaved.
My cat is very sweet.
My cat is — Ack! Wait! I
Have to fix that. Bye.)

* * *

Achos ac Effaith (Welsh)
D'on i ddim yn adnabod fy nhad i,
Felly, nawr, dw i'n galw dyn yn "ddady."

(*Cause and Effect*
I didn't know my father,
So, now, I call a man "daddy.")

POSSIBILITIES IN POETRY — AN ESSAY FOR THE COMMITTED ENTHUSIAST

Introduction

Literary movements of the twentieth century and some trends in poetry of the nineteenth century have left a legacy of confusion about what poetry has been and can be. This confusion is especially pronounced when the subjects of 1) meter and other sound effects and 2) subject matter, length, and rhetorical style are considered.

Meter and Other Sound Effects

According to Annie Finch, writing in 2014 in the *Everyman's Library* poetry anthology *Measure for Measure*, "[i]t has long been difficult to find contemporary poems written in any meter besides iambic, because metrical distinctions were so obscured during the free-verse domination that characterized most of the twentieth century (Finch and Oliver 2015: 13)." Many possibilities for poetic structure have thus been largely forgotten in the past century and, as Finch notes, this great forgetting has generally been driven by the attitudes of Free Verse enthusiasts. There was never any natural reason that Free Verse and metrical poetry could not exist side by side without conflict, but, at its inception, Free Verse was billed as a rebellion against meter instead of a new innovation in writing (cf. below) and its promoters have thus long decried meter. The Free Verse movement opened new avenues for written forms, but, in its pursuit of promoting a brand based on rebellion against what it perceived to be the establishment, it has reduced the public understanding of metrical verse to a simplistic straw man.

In conversation, someone once expressed the belief to me that, of the readers of poetry, there are two types: one that only enjoys poetic writing entirely devoid of meter and rhyme and one that is drawn to the unwavering iambic pentameter rhyming couplets of *The Canterbury Tales* (cf. Robinson 1957: 1-265). The belief is that poetry either lacks meter completely or follows an extremely rigid and simple pattern. If one reads the entry on "Free Verse" in the Encyclopaedia

Britannica, one gets the same impression. The Encyclopaedia Britannica entry begins (*Encyclopaedia Britannica* 2023, s. v. "Free Verse"):

"[F]ree verse [is] poetry organized to the cadences of speech and image patterns rather than according to a regular metrical scheme. It is 'free' only in a relative sense. It does not have the steady, abstract rhythm of traditional poetry; its rhythms are based on patterned elements such as sounds, words, phrases, sentences, and paragraphs, rather than on the traditional prosodic units of metrical feet per line. Free verse, therefore, eliminates much of the artificiality and some of the aesthetic distance of poetic expression and substitutes a flexible formal organization suited to the modern idiom and more casual tonality of the language."

The entry also later notes that the goal of Free Verse writing, as stated by the early Free Verse poets F. S. Flint, Richard Aldington, Ezra Pound, and Hilda Doolittle (the Imagists) is "to compose in sequence of the musical phrase, not in sequence of the metronome."

From a linguistic standpoint, much of this definition is meaningless (e. g., the cadence of natural speech, due to the relative nature of prosodic stress [O'Grady et al. 2010: 45], always hovers near a regular meter and even extremely regular meter is thus only minimally artificial), but this lack of meaning is not so much a reflection on Free Verse as a consequence of reliance on a misrepresentation of metrical poetry.

In general, the Britannica definition presents meter as a kind of prison from which it is beneficial to escape. However, meter is not an imposed restriction on expression like the decision to write a lipogram (a piece of writing that deliberately avoids the use of one or more specific letters [Stein and Urdang 1967, s. v. "lipogram"]). An imposed restriction would simply be an academic curiosity, but meter (as well as rhyme) holds a natural appeal to most human brains (Obermeier et al. 2013). This appeal derives from the fact that meter is a rhythm pattern built of sound alternations and is thus a form of music akin to note-free percussion (which is, notably, not the same thing as the drone of a metronome). In fact, through the late nineteenth century, the terms "poem" and "song" were used interchangeably in many cases (cf. Longfellow 1893: 348-349, Braxton 1993: 4-5, Cary and Cary 1884: preface) and they continued to be interchanged in some situations at least through the middle of the twentieth century (cf. Jackson 2013: 5-6, 77, 81, 152-153, 253, 264-265 and Rampersad and Roessel 1995: 46, 214, 451). Music is not a deliberate restriction on verbal expression. Music is another level of expression that a poet or songwriter attempts to advance at the same time as the meaning of their words. The only restriction on expression involved in the process of writing a metrical poem or a song comes from the fact that it is more difficult to say two things at once than one. Expressing an idea in words is more difficult when you are simultaneously trying to speak in the pure language of beauty: music. Meter should not be viewed as an artificial restriction on expression but an additional level of expression that can, in theory, exist without the use of meaningful sentences (think of scat jazz).

Additionally, there are several *particular* elements of the Britannica definition of Free Verse that imply a misrepresentation of metrical verse. One problematic element comes from the assertion that meter is one of the most abstract forms of rhythm. Stress, the basis of English meter, is much less abstract than phrases, sentences, and paragraphs. Stress in most dialects of English is realized through three straightforward, mechanically measurable qualities of a syllable: a stressed syllable is louder, longer, and higher-pitched than the syllables immediately adjacent to it (O'Grady et al. 2010: 45). Phrase and sentence structure are, on the other hand, much less clear in nature and their nature is consequently subject to much more controversy among linguists (cf. Carnie 2013, Hoffman and Trousdale 2013, O'Grady et al. 2010: Ch. 5, and Ritt 2004: 144-150). And paragraphs are not a property of language (which is an auditory phenomenon) at all — they are simply a visual tool for organizing long pieces of writing and writing, as every Linguistics 101 student learns, instead of being a part of language, is simply a tool for recording it (O'Grady et al. 2010: 545, Rogers 2005: 1-2). Another problematic element in the Britannica definition is the use of words like "regular" and "steady" to imply that metrical poetry cannot vary in rhythm almost at all. In practice, many poems, even those in traditional forms, vary the number of metrical feet from line to line or the types of feet within each line to create complex patterns. Both traditional ballad meter and limerick meter employ inconsistent line lengths (cf. Finch and Oliver 2015: 131-151 and Legman 1969) and, in sapphic stanzas, more than one type of foot is required *within* each line (Finch and Oliver 2015: 213-228). And, though this is an issue of the regularity of rhyme and not meter, it bears mentioning that a rhyming poem does not need to present a predictable rhyme scheme. ("Paul Revere's Ride" by Henry Wadsworth Longfellow, for example, while being thoroughly metrical and consistently rhyming, has no predictability in its rhyme distribution [cf. Longfellow 1893: 207-209].) There is an enormous amount of flexibility in the use of meter and rhyme when they are viewed as additional forms of expression advanced simultaneously with word-based meaning, rather than as arbitrary restrictions. Additionally, a final problematic element in the Britannica definition is the use of the phrases "the modern idiom" and "more casual tonality" both of which are misleading. The stress pattern of English has not changed substantially since the English Stress Rule (ESR) (and the subsequent changes its rise prompted) became dominant over the Old English Stress Rule (OESR) around five hundred years ago (Díaz-Vera 2013), so, in terms of stress-based meter, the "modern idiom" is not much different from the idiom of Shakespeare. And, while it is true that, in the English-speaking world, the past two centuries have seen a growth in alignment between the styles of poetic writing and casual speech (cf. Hollander 1993a and 1993b and Hass et al. 2000a and 2000b), there have always been casual varieties of English (as can be observed in, for example, the Mother Goose nursery rhymes [cf. *Mother Goose's Nursery Rhymes* 1877], which are centuries old [*Encyclopaedia Britannica* 2023, s. v. "Mother Goose"]) because there have always been casual situations, so the English of the present day as a whole does not exhibit a "more casual tonality" than the English of any other period. It is in fact, entirely possible to write completely metrical poems in a casual style (the light verse poems of Yip Harburg, Ogden Nash, and Dr. Seuss are clear examples, as are all the [often emotionally heavy] "dialect" poems of the late nineteenth and early twentieth centuries [cf. all or parts of Harburg 2006, Smith 2007, Geisel 1991, Riley 1993, Braxton 1993, Service 1940, Guest 1934, Honey 2006, Wilson 2000, Maxwell 2004, and Rampersad and Roessel 1995]) (cf. also below). Metrical poetry is not inherently formal in style and it does not have to sound unnatural. All in all, metrical poetry is not rooted in abstract qualities, is not restricted in expression, is not inherently rigid in form, is not antiquated in nature, and does not need to employ a high social register. These qualities may be associated with metrical poetry by some people, but they have never truly characterized it. And no poet today should be deterred from writing in meter (or rhyme) because of misconceptions. Ultimately, since they are fundamentally different forms of art, there is no more reason for Free Verse and metrical verse to compete for prestige and bookshelf space than there is for short stories and novels to do so and definitions like the one presented in *The Encyclopaedia Britannica* pick a fight that does not need to be fought.

<u>Subject Matter and Style</u>

By the time I was first taught to write poetry in elementary school during the late 1990s and early 2000s, there were already strong notions about what kind of subject matter was appropriate for poetry. I was started on short pieces of Free Verse (which, by that point, had succeeded in its rebellion against the metrical straw man it so deplored and had become the new establishment form of poetic writing) and the other students and I were consistently encouraged to write honest confessions of emotion, vivid descriptions of evocative scenes, and (occasionally) brief philosophical reflections. The length of our work was always supposed to be short and the subject matter was always supposed to be emotionally heavy. It wasn't until years later that I discovered that such limitations only began to become normalized a few centuries ago and only solidified as expectations during the latter part of the twentieth century.

In the early twentieth century, Langston Hughes proclaimed that "Poetry should treat/ Of lofty things" (Rampersad and Roessel 1995: 74), but he wrote that in a poem with the cynical title "Formula," so his awareness of the expectation should not necessarily be confused with advocacy. In contrast to Hughes's observation, however, one can observe that the definitions of the words "poem" and "poetry" in Samuel Johnson's classic dictionary from the eighteenth century contain no reference to any restriction on subject matter (or length or rhetorical style) (cf. below, where the edition is, however, from the early nineteenth century). In fact, tracing dictionary definitions of the words "poem" and "poetry" through the past few centuries provides insight into the shifting expectations of the subject matter, length, and rhetorical style of poetry that have taken us from a no-rules approach to the limitations imposed by my elementary school teachers. The following are several dictionary definitions of "poem" and/or "poetry" from dictionaries of various ages (formatting standardized by me):

A Table Alphabeticall (Robert Cawdrey, 1604):

- *Poeme* — verses of a poet.

(Cawdrey 2006, s. v. "poeme")

An Universal Etymological English Dictionary (Nathan Bailey, 1763):

- *Poem* — A piece of poetry, a composition in verse.
- *Poetry* — The art of making verses.

(Bailey 1763, s. v. "poem," "poetry")

A Dictionary of the English Language (Samuel Johnson and Henry John Todd, 1818):

- *Poem* — The work of a poet; a metrical composition.

- *Poetry* — 1. Metrical composition; the art or practice of writing poems 2. Poems; poetical pieces.

(Johnson 1994, s. v. "poem," "poetry")

American Dictionary of the English Language (Noah Webster, 1828):

- *Poem* — 1. A metrical composition; a composition in which the verses consist of certain measures, whether in blank verse or in rhyme; as the *poems* of Homer or of Milton; opposed to *prose*. 2. This term is also applied to some compositions in which the language is that of excited imagination; as the *poems* of Ossian.

● *Poetry* — 1. Metrical composition; verse; as heroic *poetry*; dramatic *poetry*; lyric or Pindaric *poetry*. 2. The art or practice of composing in verse. 3. Poems; poetical composition. 4. This term is also applied to the language of excited imagination and feeling.

(Webster 1995, s. v. "poem," "poetry")

The Oxford Universal Dictionary (1944):

● *Poem* — 1. The work of a poet, a metrical composition; a composition of words, expressing facts, thoughts, or feelings in poetical form; a piece of poetry. b. *transf.* Applied to a composition which, without the form, has some quality or qualities in common with poetry. 2. *fig.* Something (other than a composition of words) of a nature or quality akin to or likened to that of poetry.

● *Poetry* — 1. In obsolete senses: i. Equivalent to Medieval Latin *poetria* in sense of an *ars poetica.* ii. Fable, fiction. 2. In existing use:. i. The art or work of the poet. a. Composition in verse or metrical language. b. The product of this art as a form of literature; the writings of a poet or poets; poems collectively or generally; verse. (As opposed to *prose*). c. The expression of beautiful or elevated thought, imagination, or feeling, in appropriate language, such as language containing a rhythmical element and having usually a metric form. d. Extended to creative art in general (*rare*). ii. *pl.* Pieces of poetry; poems collectively (*rare*). 3. *fig.* Something compared to poetry; poetical quality, spirit, or feeling. 4. A class in Roman Catholic schools and colleges intermediate between *Syntax* and *Rhetoric.*

(Little et al. 1964, s. v. "poem," "poetry")

The Random House Dictionary of the English Language (1967):

- *Poem* — 1. A composition in verse, especially one that is characterized by a highly developed artistic form and by the use of heightened language and rhythm to express an intensely imaginative interpretation of the subject. 2. Composition which, though not in verse, is characterized by great beauty of language or thought. 3. Something having qualities that are suggestive of or likened to those of poetry.

- *Poetry* — 1. The art of rhythmical composition, written or spoken, for exciting pleasure by beautiful, imaginative, or elevated thoughts. 2. Literary work in metrical form; verse. 3. Prose with poetic qualities. 4. Poetic qualities however manifested. 5. Poetic spirit or feeling. 6. Something suggestive of or likened to poetry.

(Stein and Urdang 1967, s. v. "poem," "poetry")

Webster's Seventh New Collegiate Dictionary (1971):

- *Poem* — 1. A composition in verse. 2. A piece of poetry communicating to the reader the sense of a complete experience. 3. A creation, experience, or object likened to a poem.

- *Poetry* — 1. a. Metrical writing: verse. b. The productions of a poet: poems. 2. Writing that formulates a concentrated imaginative awareness of experience in language chosen and arranged to create a specific emotional response through meaning, sound, and rhythm. 3. a. A quality that stirs the imagination. b. A quality of spontaneity and grace.

(*Webster's Seventh New Collegiate Dictionary* 1971, s. v. "poem," "poetry")

The American Heritage Dictionary of the English Language, New Collegiate Edition (Morris 1980):

- *Poem* — 1. A composition designed to convey a vivid and imaginative sense of experience, characterized by the use of condensed language, chosen for its sound and suggestive power as well as its meaning, and by the use of such literary techniques as structured meter, natural cadences, rhyme, or metaphor. 2. Any composition in verse rather than in prose. 3. Any literary composition written with an intensity or beauty of language more characteristic of poetry than of prose: *a prose poem.* 4. Any creation, object, or experience thought to embody the lyrical beauty or structural perfection characteristic of poetry.

- *Poetry* — 1. The art or work of a poet. 2. a. Poems regarded as forming a division of literature. b. The poetic works of a given author, group, nation, or kind. 3. Any piece of literature written in meter; verse. 4. Prose that resembles a poem in form, sound, or the like. 5. The essence of or characteristic quality possessed by a poem or poems. 6. The quality of a poem or poems, as possessed by an object, act, or experience.

(Morris 1980, s. v. "poem," "poetry")

Funk and Wagnalls Standard Desk Dictionary (1984):

- *Poem* — 1. A composition in verse, characterized by the imaginative treatment of experience and a condensed use of language. 2. Any composition in verse. 3. Any composition or work of art characterized by intensity and beauty.

- *Poetry* — 1. The art or craft of writing poems. 2. Poems collectively. 3. The quality, effect, or spirit of a poem or of anything poetic. 4. Something that is poetic.

(*Funk and Wagnalls Standard Desk Dictionary*, Vol. 2 1984, s. v. "poem," "poetry")

The first dictionary cited above, Robert Cawdrey's *A Table Alphabeticall* of 1604 was the first monolingual English dictionary ever published (Cawdrey 2006: 7), so it is clear that, from the earliest attempts at defining poetry in dictionaries and for two centuries after that (at least through the 1818 edition of Johnson's dictionary), there was no restriction on the content, length, or rhetorical style of a poem or poetry. A poem was either defined as the work of a poet (a definition which offers no real clarification) or as a metrical composition, but no limitation existed on what the subject matter or style (other than, sometimes, meter) could be. Such limitless definitions never died out, but, starting in the nineteenth century, some new definitions started to be added to the original unconstrained ones and those new definitions often aimed to narrow the realm of subject matter and rhetorical style that was appropriate for poetry. This encroachment was peripheral at first (cf. Webster 1828), but, by the middle of the twentieth century, it had become a prominent element of definitions of "poem" and "poetry" (cf. Little et al. 1944, Stein and Urdang 1967, *Webster's Seventh New Collegiate Dictionary* 1971, Morris 1980, and *Funk and Wagnalls Standard Desk Dictionary* 1984). In the past two centuries, some people have thus constructed the idea that a poem must deal in certain types of subject matter or be presented within the constraints of certain length limits (note the definitions that cite condensed language as a requirement of poetry) and rhetorical styles. But such restrictions are not a fundamental aspect of poetry and are only relatively recent impositions.

Poems can deal in any type of subject matter, be of any length, and employ any rhetorical style. Poems can be funny as well as deeply emotional, can range in length from two lines (e. g., pithy couplets) to the length of a novel (cf. epic poems), and can be plain-spoken as well as highly formal and stylized. No natural limitation exists. The past two centuries have seen a narrowing of subject matter, accepted lengths, and rhetorical style, but modern poets do not need to constrain their work in these domains. The path forward in poetry, in fact, almost certainly lies in returning to an unlimited definition of what topics, lengths, and styles poetry can deal in because, otherwise, the creative options will run out. A poet, like any writer, should try to write something worth reading, but that is the only real restriction on their art in terms of content, length, tone, and word choice.

Paul Laurence Dunbar, one of the preeminent black poets of American history and, in my opinion, one of the poets whose work is most consistently of good quality, wrote both serious and humorous poems and wrote poems in both a highly formal standard style and in extreme forms of vernacular English (including his local Ohio dialect and the African American English of his time) (cf. Braxton 1993). And, importantly, Dunbar's choice of levity or gravity in his subject matter did not correspond to his choice of formality in style as can be seen by comparing the following of his poems: "Weltschmerz" (serious content, formal tone), "Theology," (humorous content, formal tone), "Long Ago" (serious content, vernacular dialect), and "Possum" (humorous content, vernacular dialect) (Braxton 1993: 220-221, 106, 192-193, 141-142). When considering the potential range of seriousness, rhetorical style, and dialect choice and the vast possibilities of mixing and matching the different variations of the three, the modern poet can learn a lot from Dunbar. And one should never forget that a poem can run for many thousands of words and tell a story, as do Layamon's *Brut* (cf. Madden 1847), Geoffrey Chaucer's *The Canterbury Tales* (cf. Robinson 1957: 1-265), John Lydgate's *Troy Book* (cf. Bergen 1906 and 1908), Edmund Spenser's *The Faerie Queene* (cf. Roche and O'Donnell 1978), Sir Walter Scott's *Marmion* (cf. Robertson 1904: 89-206), Henry Wadsworth Longfellow's *The Song of Hiawatha* (cf. Longfellow 1893: 113-164), and Lord Tennyson's *Idylls of the King* (cf. Gray 1996).

Conclusion

Ultimately, it is my hope that the art of poetry will enjoy a resurgence in popularity in the coming decades and I believe that one of the best ways to facilitate such a resurgence will be for poets to bear in mind the two main points of this essay: First, meter, rhyme, and other sound effects can be employed in infinite combinations, are not inherently restrictive, and offer poets ways of expressing themselves musically. And, second, a poet should not feel an obligation to restrict the subject matter, length, or rhetorical style of their poems in any way. With these considerations in mind, modern poets have unlimited possibilities for creativity and their work can usher in a renaissance of poetry in the twenty-first century. The future is ours for the inventing and there are many ways to move forward. Let us take full advantage of the possibilities.

Benjamin Cannicott Shavitz
New York, NY
June, 2023

<u>References</u>

Bailey, Nathan. *An Universal Etymological English Dictionary*, 20th ed. London, United Kingdom: n. p.

Bergen, Henry, ed. *Lydgate's Troy Book*, Vol. 1. London, United Kingdom: Early English Text Society, 1906.

Bergen, Henry, ed. *Lydgate's Troy Book*, Vol. 2. London, United Kingdom: Early English Text Society, 1908.

Braxton, Joanne M., ed. *The Collected Poetry of Paul Laurence Dunbar*. Charlottesville, VA and London, United Kingdom: University of Virginia Press, 1993.

Carnie, Andrew. *Syntax: A Generative Introduction*, 3rd ed. Malden, MA: Wiley-Blackwell, 2013.

Cary, Alice and Phoebe Cary. *The Poetical Works of Alice and Phoebe Cary*, Household ed. Boston, MA: Houghton, Mifflin, and Company, 1884.

Cawdrey, Robert. *The First English Dictionary 1604: Robert Cawdrey's A Table Alphabetical*. Oxford, United Kingdom: Bodleian Library, 2006.

Díaz-Vera, Javier E. "Stress Change and Phonological Variation in Early Modern English, British and American." *Jezikoslovlje* 14, no. 1 (2013): 33-46.

Encyclopaedia Britannica, s. v. "Free Verse." Chicago: Encyclopaedia Britannica, 2023.
https://www.britannica.com/art/free-verse (accessed June 6, 2023).

Encyclopaedia Britannica, s. v. "Mother Goose." Chicago: Encyclopaedia Britannica, 2023.
https://www.britannica.com/topic/Mother-Goose-fictional-character (accessed June 7, 2023).

Finch, Annie and Alexander Oliver, eds. *Measure for Measure: An Anthology of Poetic Meters (Everyman's Library Pocket Poets)*. New York/London/Toronto: Alfred A. Knopf, 2015.

Funk and Wagnalls Standard Desk Dictionary, Vol. 2. New York, NY: Harper and Row, 1984.

Geisel, Theodor. *Six by Seuss: A Treasury of Dr. Seuss Classics*. New York, NY: Random House, 1991.

Gray, J. M., ed. *Alfred, Lord Tennyson: Idylls of the King*. London, United Kingdom and New York, NY: Penguin, 1996.

Guest, Edgar A. *Collected Verse of Edgar A. Guest*. Chicago, IL: Contemporary Books, 1934.

Harburg, Edgar Yipsel. *Rhymes for the Irreverent*. Madison, WI: The Freedom from Religion Foundation, 2006.

Hass, Robert, John Hollander, Carolyn Kizer, Nathaniel Mackey, and Marjorie Perloff, eds. *American Poetry: The Twentieth Century*, Vol. 1. New York, NY: The Library of America, 2000a.

Hass, Robert, John Hollander, Carolyn Kizer, Nathaniel Mackey, and Marjorie Perloff, eds. *American Poetry: The Twentieth Century*, Vol. 2. New York, NY: The Library of America, 2000b.

Hoffman, Thomas and Graeme Trousdale, eds. *The Oxford Handbook of Construction Grammar*. Oxford, United Kingdom: Oxford University Press, 2013.

Hollander, John, ed. *American Poetry: The Nineteenth Century*, Vol. 1. New York, NY: The Library of America, 1993a.

Hollander, John, ed. *American Poetry: The Nineteenth Century*, Vol. 2. New York, NY: The Library of America, 1993b.

Honey, Maureen, ed. *Shadowed Dreams: Women's Poetry of the Harlem Renaissance*, 2nd ed., revised and expanded. New Brunswick, NJ and London, United Kingdom: Rutgers University Press, 2006.

Jackson, Major, ed. *Countee Cullen: Collected Poems*. New York, NY: The Library of America, 2013.

Johnson, Samuel. *A Dictionary of the English Language*, abridged from H. J. Todd's Corrected and Enlarged Quarto ed. by Alexander Chalmers, Barnes and Noble reprint ed. New York, NY: Barnes and Noble Books, 1994.

Legman, G., ed. *The Limerick: 1700 Examples, with Notes, Variants and Index*. New York, NY: Bell Publishing, 1969.

Little, William, H. M. Fowler, and J. Coulson, eds. *The Oxford Universal Dictionary on Historical Principles*, 3rd ed. revised with addenda by C. T. Onions. Oxford, United Kingdom: Oxford University Press, 1964.

Longfellow, Henry Wadsworth. *The Complete Poetical Works of Longfellow*. Boston, MA: Houghton Mifflin, 1893.

Madden, Sir Frederic, ed. *Layamon's Brut, Chronicle of Britain: A Poetical Semi-Saxon Paraphrase of the Brut of Wace* (in three volumes). London, United Kingdom: The Society of Antiquaries of London, 1847.

Maxwell, William J., ed. *Complete Poems: Claude McKay*. Urbana, IL and Chicago, IL: University of Illinois Press, 2004.

Morris, William, ed. *The American Heritage Dictionary of the English Language*, New Collegiate ed. Boston, MA: Houghton Mifflin, 1980.

Mother Goose's Nursery Rhymes: A Collection of Alphabets, Rhymes, Tales, and Jingles. London, United Kingdom and New York, NY: George Routledge and Sons, 1877.

Obermeier, Christian, Winfried Menninghaus, Martin von Koppenfels, Tim Raettig, Maren Schmidt-Kassow, Sascha Otterbein, and Sonja A. Kotz. "Aesthetic and Emotional Effects of Meter and Rhyme in Poetry." *Frontiers in Psychology* 4 (2013): article 10.

O'Grady, William, John Archibald, Mark Aronoff, and Janie Rees-Miller, eds. *Contemporary Linguistics: An Introduction*, 6th ed. Boston and New York: Bedford/ St. Martin's, 2010.

Rampersad, Arnold and David Roessel, eds. *The Collected Poems of Language Hughes*, First Vintage Classics ed. New York, NY: Vintage Classics, 1995.

Riley, James Whitcomb. *The Complete Poetical Works of James Whitcomb Riley*. Bloomington, IN and Indianapolis, IN: Indiana University Press, 1993.

Ritt, Nikolaus. *Selfish Sounds and Linguistic Evolution: A Darwinian Approach to Language Change*. Cambridge, United Kingdom: Cambridge University Press, 2004.

Robertson, J. Logie, ed. *The Poetical Works of Sir Walter Scott*. London, United Kingdom: Oxford University Press, 1904.

Robinson, F. N., ed. *The Works of Geoffrey Chaucer*, 2nd ed. Boston, MA: Houghton Mifflin, 1957.

Roche, Thomas P., Jr. and C. Patrick O'Donnell, Jr., eds. *Edmund Spenser: The Faerie Queene*. London, United Kingdom and New York, NY: Penguin Books, 1978.

Rogers, Henry. *Writing Systems: A Linguistic Approach*. Malden, MA: Blackwell, 2005.

Service, Robert. *Collected Poems of Robert Service*. New York, NY: G. P. Putnam's Sons, 1940.

Smith, Linell Nash, ed. *The Best of Ogden Nash*. Chicago, IL: Ivan R. Dee, 2007.

Stein, Jess and Laurence Urdang, eds. *The Random House Dictionary of the English Language*, Unabridged ed. New York, NY: Random House, 1967.

Webster, Noah. *Noah Webster's First Edition of An American Dictionary of the English Language*, Facsimile ed. San Francisco, CA: Foundation for American Christian Education, 1995.

Webster's Seventh New Collegiate Dictionary. Springfield, MA: G. and C. Merriam Company, 1971.

Wilson, Sondra Kathryn, ed. *James Weldon Johnson: Complete Poems.* London, United Kingdom and New York, NY: Penguin Books, 2000.